The Three Keys to Contentment

"Marcia has distilled the essence of Eastern and Western wisdom that will generate much thought about the meaning and goal of one's life. Both the Buddhist concept of acceptance and transcendence and Jesus' teaching about forgiveness do not imply forgetfulness, but rather learning from the past and yielding any claims it might have on your future…Inner peace comes from knowing that one is loved by our Creator, that life has a purpose, and that contentment is derived from satisfaction and fulfillment. Before one can look at the world, one must first look within in order to discover this. *The Three Keys to Contentment* will be a helpful guide to this awareness."
—The Rev. Dr. Harry L. Serio, pastor, theologian, author of *The Dwelling Place of Wonder*

"The gently delivered material, which is filled with love and compassion…is offered as a simple, accessible guide for modern life…I love the book and can think of a dozen people I'd like to hand it to, today."
—Sarajane Williams, MA, licensed psychologist, CCM, VAHT, editor, *The Harp Therapy Journal*

"Marcia portrays a unique and creative approach for looking at one's life; the past, the present and the future. In allowing yourself to open your heart and to embark upon her journey, you may find the answers to the many questions for which you are searching."
—Samantha Wesner, MSN, CRNP, RNC, nurse practitioner and wellness enthusiast

"Marcia is a skillful intuitive who has compassionately and clearly laid out a genuinely helpful book for those who become interested in awakening to inner guidance in the midst of life."
—Wali Ali Meyer, Universal Sufi master
and co-author of *Physicians of the Heart*

"*The Three Keys to Contentment* opened my eyes to the substantial abilities we already have inside us. Because of this book, I now recognize the keys in my own life and know how to use them."
—Jan McGinley Bubbenmoyer, author of
The Tree of Love and visual stylist

THE
THREE KEYS TO
CONTENTMENT

*Unlocking Your
Past, Present, and Future*

Marcia Rowe

Epigraph Books
Rhinebeck, New York

Cover design, book design and illustrations by Marcia Rowe

Visit the website:
www.thethreekeystocontentment.com

Library of Congress Control Number: 2016933613
ISBN # 978-1-944037-21-5

Printed in the United States of America

Epigraph Books
22 East Market Street, Suite 304
Rhinebeck, NY 12572
(845) 876-4861
www.epigraphps.com

DEDICATION

To my spiritual teacher,

Wali Ali Meyer,

with gratitude

for his encouragement

and guidance

*"In oneself lies the whole world,
and if you know how to look and learn,
then the door is there and the key is in your hand.
Nobody on earth can give you either
that key or the door to open,
except yourself."*

J. Krishnamurti, universal spiritual teacher

Marcia,
May the Three Keys
be helpful to you.
Love, Marcia Rosie

CONTENTS

INTRODUCTION

Three little antique keys

Keys, locks, doorknobs, and antique hardware in general have been a fascination of mine for over forty years. I have boxes of keys, old locks, doorknobs, and hinges in the attic. Framed displays of antique locks and keys hang on my walls. Mounted ornate doorknobs sit on my shelves. Keys are a theme in my artwork. And one of the reasons I decided to buy my 1870's farmhouse was that the original hardware was still on all the doors.

For the past twenty-five years, I have been wearing three antique furniture keys on a necklace chain. At first I just liked their look. Later, I realized they had the deeper meaning of owning the keys to my life ~ a symbol of personal empowerment.

I wore the three keys necklace to a spiritual retreat at a mountaintop camp in the summer of 2000. When a friend asked about the meaning, I told her they symbolized *The Past, Present, and Future.* "But what *are* the keys to the past, present, and future?" she asked. After years of wearing the keys I never thought about it that way before.

As I walked down a wooded path I asked the Spirit of Guidance for help with this question. Very quickly the answer was clear.

The Key to the Past is Forgiveness.

The Key to the Present is Gratitude.

The Key to the Future is Faith.

Later, when I returned home, I started to ponder ~ if these are the keys, what are the locks? Again, the answer was clear.

The Lock on the Past is Regret.

The Lock on the Present is Self-pity.

The Lock on the Future is Fear.

As my life's daily challenges presented themselves I would find myself in some state of discontent. A painful memory revisited. A project canceled. A worry about tomorrow's losses.

I could now see myself being *locked* into negative thoughts about the past, present, and future. This was the cause of my suffering. Viewing my life as a series of regrets certainly was depressing. Feeling self-pity because my current situation was less than ideal was robbing me of energy. Fearing the worst possible outcomes was making the future a very scary place.

I started to consciously change my focus to *the keys* instead of the locks. Forgiving others and myself when mistakes of the past came to mind. Practicing gratitude for all the good things around me when disappointments came. Imagining success and the ability to handle whatever would come my way.

One winter night in 2010 I had a vivid dream and awoke with clear words in my mind ~ *Write about the Three Keys.*

I knew I had to follow the Spirit of Guidance and begin the process of writing for my own understanding. Perhaps the ideas would be useful to others as well.

For many years I was using a writing technique to get answers to life's troubling questions. I would get myself into a meditative state through prayer and visualization and then write down my question of the moment.

A single word would come to mind and I would write it down. Then words began to flow and I continued to write what I heard. I never had any idea of where the message would take me. I just concentrated on listening for the next sentence and on it flowed until pages were filled with answers.

The wisdom and comfort of the words always touched my heart and filled me with peace. The speed and organization of the writing amazed me because my normal process is slow and labored.

This is the method, with later editing, that I have used to write about *The Three Keys to Contentment.* I have discovered it is the book *I* really needed to read, and read again.

I do not claim to be able to stay *unlocked* every day. I struggle with regret at times and I compare myself to others way too often. Fear can get a fierce grip on me. But now I know I have the *keys* to my discontent which can open my life to a state of contentment. I just have to remember to use them, daily.

I hope you find the insights in *The Three Keys to Contentment* helpful in your *own* search for contentment.

Marcia

The purpose of the book:

**To enlighten the reader
to the simple truths of living.**

Complexity does not bring clarity;
only simplicity will bring the truth to light and to life.
The message is brief;
the explanations can go on forever.

Forgiveness * Gratitude * Faith

All else will flow from the results of
these powerful thought forms.

Keys and Contentment

KEYS AND CONTENTMENT

The symbolism of keys

Many people find an attraction to the key as a symbol of success.

Keys represent the solutions to a problem; the answer to a riddle, the opening of a treasure box.

Keys are golden or silver to add to the impression of value. Precious gems add even more to the allure of secret treasure uncovered. If the keys themselves are bejeweled, how rich must be the contents of the box.

Keys have a connection to royalty as well. Kings gave the keys to trusted advisors who oversaw the wealth of the kingdom. This signified great confidence in the wisdom and morals of the subjects. To be given the keys implies you are worthy of trust and honor.

Keys have always held power as a visual statement; the keys to the kingdom, the key to the city, the key to the heart. Those who hold the keys hold the power.

This is why it is important to hold your own keys to the past, present, and future, not waiting till someone else opens the doors to contentment. It is an inside job. The only way through the doors is to unlock them yourself. Waiting for external circumstances to be perfect is an illusion. There will always be trials and adversity so long as one is on the earth plane. But to find contentment *in spite of* the trials is to succeed at life in the deepest way.

Keys also represent safety. To have the keys implies others are not able to compromise security. Things are locked up in safekeeping until the proper keys are used. Locks and keys together provide a system of protection from intruders. Our inner life is our own. We do not have to share this world with everyone. The keys can be used by us when desired, not when requested by others.

Keys will always hold a fascination for their symbolism of power and discovery.

The goals of life

Everyone desires happiness although the form that this takes is as varied as humanity itself. Each person has innate talents, gifts, and longings forming their natural desires. Going through life without realizing one's calling is a struggle indeed. Once the path is discovered the challenges continue, but the rewards follow as well.

But there is another higher goal that many seek: a longing for fulfillment and peace. There comes a time in one's life to follow the inner journey. All the instincts focus the mind on the highest calling ~ a connection with the Divine Source.

This process of finding one's path to union is the way of all mystics, seekers, and sages. Volumes have been written about the best way to achieve enlightenment, salvation, ego-annihilation. However one proceeds, the end result is the same ~ a state of bliss that comes from within.

Outer forms give us happiness;
inner space gives us joy.

Contentment

Contentment is being able to be satisfied with what is happening now. Not what the ideal version would be, could be, should be, but what is actually occurring. This is the only version available to you right now. Longing for the ideal robs you of what is good in the moment. Perfection is an illusion that shimmers and shines but proves elusive. Hold on to what is real instead ~ what is right in front of you. Longing for what is *not* here robs you of precious moments that cannot be replaced.

Why focus on lack? Focus on the abundance that surrounds you. The natural world has pleasures nothing can rival. Just look up ~ the sky is available to all. Just look down ~ the earth under your feet supports us all. Find a stream flowing with life-giving water. Stare into a fire and see the power of energy.

Find contentment within yourself, for all outer forms are temporary, ever changing, and open to decay. The internal world is the realm of the eternal.

Holding on to that which will end provides temporary relief but ultimately fails to satisfy. We know that the world, which seems so permanent, is constantly changing. The climate is always in flux, which affects all living things.

Be not concerned with form.
That which is eternal is internal.

The difference between happiness and contentment

Contentment is a deep feeling of acceptance of all of life's phases, the ups and downs, the good and bad. It is a mature understanding of the world and all its challenges. Contentment brings a sense of peace in that all is in perfect Divine order. Our own ideas of perfection may be challenged, but we see the bigger picture or at least we *trust* there is a bigger picture.

Happiness is momentary. Contentment is lasting. We can have experiences of great happiness when good things come our way ~ a new love interest, a great new job, the birth of a child ~ all bring the feelings of happiness. But life moves on to the next challenges, settling into the daily routine. Happiness is hard to sustain and may even cause unhappiness because of its fleeting nature.

The grasping for the elusive butterfly of happiness
often leaves us empty-handed.

Rather seek for contentment for it can be secured. It is more within our control. Outer events cause the feelings of happiness. Inner practices cause the feelings of contentment. What is outside our control makes us feel powerless and anxious. We cannot control much of what comes to us daily; however, we can control our re-action to it.

The Three Keys open the doors to contentment by giving the power to the user. No longer locked into negative states of being, the way is open to a more positive view of life. The only way to stay in happiness is by trying to control circumstances and other people. This is an impossible task and usually brings unhappiness to those around us and frustration to ourselves.

> *"It is better to put on sandals*
> *than to try to carpet the world."*
> Hindu saying

The way to stay in contentment is to control our thoughts and in turn our emotions and actions. This is within our power and therefore we feel more confidence in our ability to cope with life.

Manifesting results through positive thinking

There is only one path to freedom and it is created in the mind. Believing that there is an opening makes it so. Whatever one can dream, one can achieve. Therefore, it is incumbent upon us to remain open to all thoughts of success. Limited thoughts are just that; limitations to what can be achieved. Without restrictions the mind can travel to distant shores, unencumbered by the rules of time and space; all is possible. It is in this realm that everything begins.

First the thought, then the word, then the feeling, then the action, then the result. This is how it ever has been and shall be, unto eternity.

> *"Spirit is the Life, Mind is the Builder and*
> *the Physical is the Result."*
> Edgar Cayce, psychic and father of holistic medicine

Following in the Creator's image, we can achieve no less. We limit ourselves to a narrow path when the whole world is ours. Being open to all that our dreams show us is possible is the real challenge. Our doubts and fears restrict the outcome while our hopes empower the outcome.

The power of the mind

Life is the result of the repetition of thoughts. That may be a startling statement, but it is true. When one dwells on a thought, positive or negative, an energy force is created.

The repetition of the thought empowers it into action. Believing that good or ill are coming one's way causes the very result one longs for or fears. Therefore, thoughts are powerful forces that need to be respected. Spiritual traditions are built on the concept of mind control as a means to a place of peace and equanimity. When one controls one's own mind, one has true mastery.

> *"A monk who is skilled in concentration*
> *can cut the Himalayas in two."*
> Buddha

Being open to lessons of self-control leads to greater riches than one can imagine. There is something magical about the power of concentrated thought. The effect of group prayer is a demonstration of this principal. When many focus their thoughts continually on a positive outcome, that is the actual result. The power of repetition, in numbers of people and in numbers of thoughts, is substantial. This can be seen in stories of rescues and healings. Visualizations add to the power for even stronger results.

Toxic thoughts

Letting the mind wander into negative territory is dangerous indeed. Fears of calamity can provoke calamity. Allowing worry to take hold will create an opening for negative consequences to occur. The mind can conjure up all manner of disasters. Calling up these images creates an imprint that can be filled in.

"So don't be anxious about tomorrow. God will take care of your tomorrow, too. Live one day at a time."
Jesus

Something negative happens and people say, "That was my worst fear," yet they don't see the connection between thought and result. Allowing our minds to flow into negative territory is dangerous for us and those around us. The dark energy can take hold in a family, a neighborhood, or a country, and the fear produced will multiply the darkness. This is the downfall of individuals and societies. As the individual is overcome with fear and hopelessness, so too is the culture.

Therefore, limit the intake of negative subject matter in books, TV, movies and the internet. There is a large audience for this because it excites a deep survival center in the brain. Young men especially are attracted to this type of excitement, for they are often asked to participate in dangerous conditions ~ as police officers, soldiers, and rescue workers.

For the rest of us it is best to refrain from indulging in the dark world of violence and sexual corruption. It pulls down the whole society by tipping the balance of light and dark energies.

Stay focused on things beautiful, harmonious, and full of love. Then your life will be full of these things in mind, body, and spirit. There is a reason that the world's spiritual teachings emphasize this mind control, for without it we are lost to the power of darkness.

> *"Finally brothers and sisters, whatever is true,*
> *whatever is noble, whatever is right,*
> *whatever is pure, whatever is lovely, whatever*
> *is admirable ~ if anything is excellent or praiseworthy*
> *~ think about such things."*
> Paul, Apostle of Jesus

Three reasons to use The Three Keys

Life presents challenges daily to our emotional health. Practicing the Three Keys on a regular basis brings stability. Those who are flooded by feelings of regret, self-pity, and fear cannot rise to the occasion when new challenges appear. Keeping a clean house emotionally allows us to focus on what is arising now.

Family and friends will appreciate the improved nature of the relationships and our happier selves. We lighten the load for everyone when we lighten our own.

Our relationship with the Divine is strengthened. Daily connection helps us feel supported when hard times come. And we are more sensitive to inner guidance.

*Release * Embrace * Go forth.*

The Emotional House

This concept becomes the foundation of *The Three Keys'* healing practice. Imagine an illustration of doorways to the subconscious, conscious, and superconscious. This helps one see the progression, the rising in consciousness.

Go from the lower level where pain is buried beneath life's everyday activity. Rise up to awareness of all that surrounds one in beauty and harmony. Ascend to the highest realm of love where all things are possible.

The Emotional House is the construct that enables you to see the levels of awareness with clarity and simplicity. Then you know at what level you are working.

The Past is the foundation for today and tomorrow. It must be cleared of old issues that weaken the stability of the house. Forgiveness is the process of releasing people from our past. Ideally, the basement is empty of all beings but ourselves. Ironically, sometimes the hardest person to forgive *is* our self. Without self-forgiveness we stay wounded and stuck in the past.

The Present is spacious, bright, full of beauty, if we just open our eyes to see. This room allows for humor, creativity, friendship, community, giving and receiving, play and work, all that life offers to us for growth. Go into the world with wonder, with the eyes of a child. See the diversity of life in plants, animals, rocks, trees, fishes and seas. This planet is amazing and unique in the universe. Don't fail to appreciate the marvel that it is and your unique place in it. You are where you are for a purpose, and to discover that purpose is life's mysterious challenge. Those who find it are blessed indeed for they find peace of mind. Don't give up the search, it is worth the effort. Go in peace. Go within. Go without.

The Future rises above us as in a vision. All the hopes and fears hover there waiting to be manifested. Gifts of the future must be unwrapped, the ribbons to the past must be cut, the box opened. No one who has succeeded in making their dreams come true has remained unchanged. The two are not compatible. Longing for dreams without letting go of the present is like trying to be in two places at once. You cannot go to Paris without leaving your home town. This is the physical reality and spiritual reality as well. Buy a ticket to the future and then get ready to move upward toward your destination.

Hope and faith are the currency of change.

"Look not mournfully into the past. It comes not back again. Wisely improve the present. It is thine. Go forth to meet the shadowy future without fear."
Henry Wadsworth Longfellow, poet

The Lock
on the Past:
REGRET

REGRET SAYS:

"I can't stop thinking about the mistakes I made."

"Other people always let me down. I can't trust *anyone*."

"I can't sleep whenever I remember trouble from the past."

"I have failed so many times and now I *am* a failure."

"My decisions were poor, time and time again."

"My life would be so different now, *if only…*"

"It is so painful to think of the past."

"I can *never* forgive him for what he did."

"I will *never* be free of the pain of the past."

"My whole life is a failure."

REGRET

The lock on the past is regret.

To *re*gret is to *re*consider actions taken; to see the consequence of the path taken; to wish for another chance at life. We see clearly, from today's perspective, what was helpful and what was hurtful. All actions have consequences ~ some short-term, some long-term. Those that cause the greatest regret have the longest reach into the future. Life-changing decisions are often made with little thought of the harmful potential. Great expectations can be followed by even greater disappointments. Making good decisions is central to a satisfying life. But it is a learning process and we need to be gentle with ourselves.

Regret is an underlying sadness that blankets the ability to feel joy in the present moment. It makes the days long and the nights even longer. Constantly looking back at the errors of the past puts the focus on what is wrong instead of what is right. Regret means you are *always* saying you are sorry. You are sorry for what you did. Sorry for what he or she did not do. Sorry for how life turned out in general.

Mistakes will be made, the pain of loss will come, opportunities will be missed ~ this is the challenge of life on earth. No one is immune to the struggle forward through difficulties. They can happen daily. There is nothing to be gained from dwelling on the regrets. Turn them into moments of learning instead. Analyze the situations, looking for patterns of faulty thinking that keep repeating. See the links between thoughts, actions, and outcomes.

There is much to be learned from our mistakes.

Believe all things work together to build a life of character, of substance, of beauty, even in the ashes. The hard times make the good times all the better. The sour makes the sweet even sweeter.

The heaviness of regret

Regret is the baggage that holds us back from enjoying the present moment. Reliving past mistakes and betrayals robs us of the ability to see the opportunities for happiness that are occurring today. Always looking over our shoulder to the past allows us to stumble over today's possibilities.

Regret is like a rope that is tied around the waist pulling us backward. It takes much more energy to go forward when there is so much pull from the past. Some rope is so thick and heavy that life is lived in total regret ~ there is no joy in the present or hope for the future. The weight of the disastrous past has tipped the balance of life completely. A severe shock to one's system through violence, illness or death can create an enormous burden to the soul.

Carrying the heavy stones of personal mistakes takes energy from the present moment. To be free to begin new adventures, we must be able to release the mistakes of the past for no progress can be made without also making mistakes. They are a sign that new things are being attempted, beyond the comforts of the familiar. All things have the potential for success or failure. To dwell on past failures limits the potential for success in the future. Focus instead on the wide-open possibilities for achieving your goals. Create a new groove in your mind's pathway ~ one of optimism and hopefulness.

> *"Tribe follows tribe and nation follows nation, like waves of the sea. It is the order of nature and regret is useless."*
> Chief Seattle, Native American orator

When life is full of regret, the past replaces the present and the natural order of life is reversed. Like a car going only backward, the destination can never be reached. The focus must always be on the present with the future on the horizon. Traveling through life is challenging enough with one's hands on the wheel of the present. To constantly look backward creates unnecessary stress and confusion. The present moment is the only time to make the next good decision. Learn from the past, forgive the past, release the past, and find the path forward from this precious present moment.

What could have been

Regret for how things might have been if only tragedy had not struck is difficult indeed. The pain of loss can go on for years, unchanging, unyielding. A heart broken by loss may never be completely repaired, but it can be mended. Allowing the pain to overcome all beauty in life is to suffer every day for what is in the past. The present moment is where healing can happen.

Some crimes, accidents, and illnesses alter life in an instant. Life can never be the same. The scene can be replayed over and over, but the outcome is the same. There is no opportunity to make different decisions. What is done is done. Regret can perpetually ask *why* and say *if only*, keeping the pain of the past moment ongoing in the present.

Grieving

Regret has a sadness, heaviness, and loneliness to it. Grieving is a form of regret for what is finished and cannot happen again. Replaying the slide show of the mind keeps us stuck in memories. There is a time for grief. Letting go is difficult. But there is also a time to move on and begin again.

Some painful memories keep us attached to loved ones, and letting go can feel like forgetting. The pain becomes the link to the past. Honor their memory with thoughts of happy times instead. Replace the pain with peace.

Breathe in peace. Breathe out peace.

Listen to the inner voice that guides us toward wholeness, connection, and love. There is no higher calling.

High ideals

Regret is created when one's actions do not live up to one's ideals. It is easy to hold high standards for one's self and others, but it not easy to follow them. Mistakes will be made. It is human to err. Only God is perfect.

The ideals keep us striving forward, always trying to rise to the highest plane of thoughts, words, and actions. The emotions are the wild card in the game of life. Past hurts and self-protection lead to emotional fragility which can be pierced by words or actions of others. Then, one's own nature goes into defense and anger. Regrets follow, for now emotions have trumped reason and hurts have trumped love.

Stagnation

Living with regret and not taking actions to make amends where possible leads to depression, stagnation, and even illness. It stops creativity. It stops hope. It stops the flow of life. There is one direction to be pointed in life and it is forward. Allowing the mind to dwell in the past keeps the energy low for life's new ventures. The past is complete and nothing can undo what is done. The way is ahead of you *not* behind you.

There is nothing to be gained from focus on regret. Life moves on, seasons change, and we must change as well. Nothing that is alive is static. Everything is moving. Movement *is* life.

Trying to change the past

Everyone has moments in life's long story that we wish we could change. It is natural to want the best outcomes in all areas of our lives. When we repeatedly focus on the mistakes and the "*if only*" responses, we give great power to the past. It has happened and it cannot be altered.

> *"For even God lacks this one thing alone,*
> *to make a deed that has been done undone."*
> Agathon, Greek poet

Science fiction aside, it is not possible to change the course of history by going backward. And only by breathing beauty into the present moment can we change the future. We are spinning our wheels and going nowhere if the errors of the past are the focus of our energies.

Releasing the past

Believing in a Higher Power helps to release the past. The story of one's life is told in successes and failures, blessings and challenges, pleasures and pains. Each season has its reason. Sometimes we can only see the pattern of perfection from a great distance. Time reveals the purpose for the struggles.

Allow for lessons to be learned ~ be open to the possibility that everything happens exactly as it should ~ not for our happiness but for our personal growth.

The past teaches us lessons and helps us improve. The past reveals patterns of actions and responses that help us make better decisions today. And the past is meant to be reviewed, not regretted.

> *"It is the nature of things,*
> *that joy arises in a person free from remorse."*
> Buddha

The Key
to the Past:
FORGIVENESS

FORGIVENESS SAYS:

"I *can* release the pain of the past."

"Holding onto anger toward others only poisons me.
I let it go."

"I can accept that the past has created the present and
lessons were learned."

" I *can* forgive myself for poor decisions made by my
inexperienced younger self."

"Others acted in selfish ways and did not intend
to harm me in the process."

"Life is short. I need to focus on *today* and let the past rest."

"I release all hurts, slights, and losses
and find peace *now*."

"I do not condone the bad actions of others, but I release
my anger and pain."

"I am bigger than the problems of the past."

"Love *can* overcome pain."

FORGIVENESS

The key to the past is forgiveness.

There is nothing that cannot be forgiven. Nothing at all. Although life presents pain and suffering as the consequence of error, the emotional results can be changed. Forgiveness is the celestial path to healing. Being open to the possibility of a clean slate opens the door to freedom. Guilt and shame bind us to our lower natures. Forgiveness raises the level of vibration ~ clearing the heaviness that keeps us tied to old patterns of being and doing. See that all things are possible. The past is not the keeper of the future. You can begin again each day with fresh insights, motives, and choices.

Be not concerned with what has gone before.
All is forgiven and washed anew.

Forgiveness opens the mind and the heart to healing. Resentments, anger, and guilt keep us stuck in the past. *What if, if only, why, why not* all replay the past looking for new outcomes. Change can only happen in the present, of course, so replaying the past goes nowhere. Release the old ways ~ let go of the images that cause pain. Clear the space in your mind and heart for new relationships.

Path to forgiveness

Letting go of all that troubles you is the key to contentment. The past is full of hurts, slights, harsh words, failures, misunderstandings, and disappointments. To hold onto this bucket of sorrow is to be weighed down in life. The burden of carrying this weight takes away the joy of the present moment. How can we relax and experience today's potential when the past errors are ever present? To be fully present in *this* moment the past needs to be cleansed and cleared.

There is a process to do this that involves opening the heart to witness the grievance once again from the place of compassion ~ for self and others. This healing practice allows the pains of the past to be turned into shadows of their former selves. Shadows are soft and without real form. They can be walked through without causing harm to us. Shadows are created when a strong light is directed at an object. The Light of Love shines on the pains of the past, purifying and transforming the hard places into soft memories.

....

*Recall a moment of pain ~ one caused by another's
thoughtlessness and need to have their own way.
Remember how they looked, where this happened, and
when it occurred. Then relive how you looked and felt
at the moment of betrayal.*

*Now replay the scene from the perspective of the
angels, seeing both parties from above. See the
wounded nature of the betrayer ~ the losses in their
life, the hurts they have endured, the pain they have
suffered. With compassion for both parties, let the
scene melt into soft focus. All hard edges of the memory
blur as compassion softens the heart.
Love is the remedy for all pain and loss.*

....

22

Of course, all loss is not created equally. Start with slights and harsh words that sting your memory. Begin with the ones that are easiest to release but do begin. The past is full of painful shards that need not cause pain in the present. Why allow these old relics to limit today's happiness?

The large wounds, of course, need large remedies. The events of deep loss and pain will take gentle, slow effort to transform into softness. Repetition will help this process as well as following inner guidance. Working around the edges of the story will soften it as well. There is no story that cannot be helped by this process.

> *"It is in pardoning that we are pardoned."*
> St. Francis of Assisi, Catholic friar

The longer the list of offenders the deeper the pull of the past is on your life and your vitality. Letting go of grudges frees you from the links to the past. The other person does not need to know of your change of heart ~ perhaps it would even cause harm to make contact Change your own heart and the relationship will change too.

Opening the heart

Moving forward with the concept of Forgiveness, we consider the places of deep hurt and shame. Letting go of the need for revenge and punishment can be a time-consuming process. Once broken, the heart is loath to open up to further damage. A hardness develops around the heart as a protection and it becomes a prison. The natural state of the heart is openness ~ yielding and soft. To be wounded in the heart is to close off the flow of love to self and others.

When one has been damaged by life's unfairness the natural reaction is self-protection. Natural, perhaps, but not always useful in the long run for all of life's joy flows through the heart. By limiting the capacity of the heart to receive the full measure of life's feelings, one is shut out from life's blessings.

Giving in to feelings of loss and despair only strengthens the shell of protection. They reinforce the world as a hard and fearsome place where one must be on guard at all times. Depression takes one deeper into self-separation from people, places, and things that might cause pain. The walls grow higher and the self grows lonelier. All in the cause of protection from pain, from regret, from the past.

> *"Forgiveness is not an occasional act,*
> *it is a constant attitude."*
> Martin Luther King, Jr., Protestant minister and activist

The antidote is forgiveness. Rather than protecting the heart by shielding it from outside influences, the solution is to open the heart. In a careful and respectful process, the heart is welcomed into a safe place where the hurts can be honored, healed, and removed. The calluses on the heart's surface are softened, allowing the tender places to be revealed once more. Only in a loving atmosphere can this process reveal the delicate nature of the loving heart.

How many beings are walking through their days with hardened hearts ~ protected but not really experiencing life's riches? What seems to be a protection from further harm is really a rejection of any joy. Open heartedness is the only way to truly feel the love that is circulating throughout the universe.

"Only a heart with wings can fly."
Hazrat Inayat Khan, Universal Sufi master and musician

There is a river of love flowing from God's heart to all who are captive to hurts of the past. Being barren and dry, the healing waters bring life abundantly. Go into the shadows of the past for there lies the Truth that will set you free. Evil lives in the darkness, but the Light always overcomes darkness as each sunrise testifies to all the earth.

Never was there a night that could resist the coming dawn.

As each person experiences hurt, a bit of darkness forms within us. It is not our own nature but the result of the pain we endured. Going into the darkness with the Light of Truth dissolves all semblance of substance. It is an illusion now, melting away as snow melts in the sunshine.

Be ever willing to see the Truth, to speak the Truth,
to be the Truth.

When seen from a high place the whole story of humanity is one of loss and love. Which side will you be on? Focusing on loss and regret or opening up to love and forgiveness? The choice is yours. The future is where hope resides. Let the past be complete and contained within the heart.

The Lock
on the Present:
SELF-PITY

SELF-PITY SAYS:

"I don't have the lucky breaks that others have."

"Why does everything go *so* hard for me?"

"Everyone else has more than me."

"Life is a struggle for me but others have it *easy*."

"All my friends are successful but I am stuck
in this job I dislike."

"I see couples everywhere but I am still alone and miserable."

"My looks are always a big disappointment."

"Why do I always have so *many* setbacks?"

"I get so angry when things don't go my way."

"I can't get what I want."

SELF-PITY

The lock on the present is self-pity.

Feeling that one is stuck in a situation that is not ideal can lead to self-pity. "Others have reached their ideals and I have not," is the sentence that causes all the trouble. For in reality very few people reach their ideals in all areas of life. Some may excel in business but suffer losses at home. Others succeed in marriage but struggle with health issues. Others long for family life and find it denied. There will always be those who have more than we do and many, many more who have much less. If we focus only on the successful few and disregard the masses, self-pity is certain to arise.

> *"Self-pity is the worst poverty; it overwhelms one until one sees nothing but illness, trouble, and pain."*
> Hazrat Inayat Khan, Universal Sufi master and musician

A *poor me* attitude brings on jealousy, envy, and anger toward others. It can lead to broken relationships, illness, and even violence. How many wars are fought because of this very feeling of *less than?* The struggle to be free is inherent in all beings, but the desire for another's life is misguided. We need to seek the highest, noblest version of *our own* life, not the cheap imitation of another's. The struggles, losses, and challenges of each life form the character and help the soul to rise higher. Shortcuts to the processes do not work. Stealing another's wife or identity or job does not bring real satisfaction. The goals must be reached honorably for success to be lasting and true.

Being at peace with our own story as it unfolds in its own timing is essential to contentment. Always strive toward your ideals but allow the process to have its own rhythms and cycles. We do not see the big picture. It is not possible. But all things work toward the highest good. Even extreme hardship has its rewards for others have been given the opportunity to help eliminate this very suffering.

There is no hierarchy in suffering. All leads to a feeling of self-pity or a rising up to the feeling of gratitude. While not the first reaction to difficult times, gratitude is the long-term solution.

Be gentle in your judgments and kind in your actions.

Self-pity is a focus on the small self that is engaged in struggle and strife. Our bodies, our minds, and our emotions are subject to limitations. Limitations leave us feeling frustrated. Frustrations lead to anger. Anger leads to hurt. And when we are hurt we feel sorry for ourselves. We feel we don't deserve this outcome. We want life to be fair. We want what others have and we lack. We want out dreams to come true, *now.*

> *"Self-pity is our worst enemy and if we yield to it,*
> *we can never do anything good in the world."*
> Helen Keller, hearing/visually impaired author and activist

Longing for what others have blocks us from seeing what we have right in front of us. Listen to your thoughts of judgment and comparison. They separate all of life into categories for competition. Each person has received what is needed to grow spiritually, to grow into dependence on the Source of All ~ to surrender to

Divine Will. This looks different for each being as we all have a story to be told.

Realize that you are exactly where you need to be. Be grateful for the challenges, the losses. They define your character and make you stronger. Ease breeds laziness. Challenges need solutions. Finding solutions stretches the mind to expand and grow. We tell children that learning in school is necessary and even fun. Yet as adults *we* want life to be easy.

Jealousy

Self-pity can lead to jealousy, a vile poison in any relationship and in our own bodies. Jealousy leads to anger, which raises our blood pressure and pumps chemicals into our bloodstream. If repeated often enough we damage our very own hearts from not being open-hearted toward others. Any negative emotion projected outward returns to us in the form of wasted energy and perhaps even illness.

> *"Resentment is like drinking poison
> and then hoping it will kill your enemies."*
> Nelson Mandela, first black president of South Africa

Thinking that others have all the breaks in life without struggle is often short-sighted. Many a glamorous, wealthy person has a story of loss and overcoming. No one is immune to life's difficulties. To think otherwise is to maintain a childish fairytale. *Happily ever after* happens in story-telling but not in real life. Real life is much more interesting.

Jealousy can put a barrier on our heart, constricting the flow of love to others. We think we are protecting ourselves from potential harm, but we are barricading ourselves in our own emotional prison.

Jealous longing for what others have does nothing to bring it to us. It only blocks the flow of love and keeps us stuck in a place of lacking. Rejoicing in others' happy state is the only way to bring the stream of happiness your way.

What creates the jealous rage that causes someone to lash out in violence? An overwhelming sense of self-pity. The lack of connection to others ~ through romantic loss, job loss, and life's cruelties ~ can break one completely.

Jealousy locks out the ability to find joy in others' success. There is pleasure in seeing friends achieve their goals, find happiness with partners, and develop their talents. Jealousy tears down those successes and leaves us alone in our suffering.

> *"The jealous are troublesome to others,*
> *but a torment to themselves."*
> William Penn, Quaker author

Self-pity and despair

Be mindful of the currents of self-pity as they swirl around you. They can carry you into despair, flowing through all thoughts of success like a flood of negativity. Loss and failure create an opening for thoughts of hopelessness. Self-pity leads to inactivity and resentment.

Taking action depends on hope and optimism. Self-pity short-circuits the process. Whenever life gives us challenges we have a choice ~ to try to overcome or to give up. Self-pity says *"Why try?" "It's too hard!" "I can't do it!"*

We revert to a childlike state of helplessness, wanting to be rescued, for mother to make it all better. This might be the first reaction but cannot be the last word. Movement forward requires that we first move beyond childish notions of being taken care of by a parent. Childhood is a time of limited responsibility and limited authority, as it should be. Children don't have the resources or understanding to resolve problems. It is a time of surrender to those in authority, trusting in their desire to do the best for us.

Of course, sometimes parents fail in their duty to protect and guide safely. There can be an abuse of power, with vulnerable children trusting the adults to do their best. How sad when trust is broken and tiny hearts are damaged. The mending process can take a lifetime. But it can be done through forgiveness of the past.

To fully be an adult, one must take responsibility for problem-solving. No longer dependent on someone else, we need to work through life's complexities using the resources available to us. We are not totally alone in this process ~ just totally responsible to do our best. Reaching out to experts, asking for advice, reading the research all aid in problem-solving. No one can know all the answers without help. Guidance is leading us toward solutions that feel solid and satisfying. The combination of personal work and help from others weaves a tight web of support. What connects us to one another makes us all stronger.

Release and be free

Letting go of self-pity frees us to reach deep inside for our inner strength. How do we know what we can accomplish if we are not tested? Being given too much can disable the maturing process, for the effort has been removed. Muscles are made through repetitive action and effort. Without use muscles atrophy and the same is true of our inner strength.

Problems are not punishments. They are exercises to build our character. Think of who is admired in our societies. It is those who have overcome great challenges ~ life-imposed or self-imposed. Whether recovering from a physical illness or climbing a dangerous mountain, the effort made inspires us. We imagine ourselves getting through our own obstacles because others have gone before us. Learn from the actions of others how to marshal your resources and then forge ahead.

"Life is full of suffering and also great overcoming."
Helen Keller, hearing/visually impaired author and activist

The Key
to the Present:
GRATITUDE

GRATITUDE SAYS:

"I *appreciate* the opportunities and the challenges of life."

"Beauty is everywhere if I look carefully."

"I am blessed to have friends and family."

"I *see* that my struggles have made me stronger."

"Every day is an opportunity to be kind."

"Life is a series of ups and downs and
I am *grateful* for the ride."

"My senses bring me pleasure every day."

"My body is a marvelous creation."

"My life is perfect in its imperfection."

"My heart expands with the thought of all my blessings."

GRATITUDE

The key to the present is gratitude.

In the present moment, gratitude is the key to all that is good and uplifting. While self-pity brings heaviness, gratitude brings a lightness of being. When you see what is positive about your circumstance even chores become blessings. You have chores because you have a full life ~ a job, a home, or a family.

When one is thankful the eyes of the heart are open. We truly see the beauty around us and feel the blessing of being alive. Go within the circumstances to see the hidden blessing. Even difficult times often have an unexpected motivation toward a new mission in life. Tragedies may ultimately create the impetus for a social movement, an environmental cause, or a personal legacy. Judge not what is good or bad for the final outcome may surprise everyone.

Gratitude is the sacred oil that lubricates life. Without this oil the everyday grinding of disappointment and stress become debilitating. Gratitude loosens up the stuck places in our hearts, smooths out the wrinkles in our mind and lets our spirit fly free.

> *"If the only prayer you said was thank you*
> *that would be enough."*
> Meister Eckhart, theologian, philosopher, and mystic

Dwelling on what is *working* rather than what is *lacking* changes the energy of relationships, organizations, and ourselves. Gratitude brings a sense of optimism that yields dividends of hope. Hope brings feelings of confidence that allow new ideas to emerge. And new ideas yield positive change. The chain of change starts from gratitude for what is available right now.

> *To deny the gifts of the present*
> *is to deny the hopes of the future.*

New awareness

Be open to new pathways and unexpected trails. The familiar paths may be well worn but new ones offer treasures among the rocks. When we are guided to try something new, gratitude is the way forward.

Open your eyes to all the blessings that surround you. This is the path to peace, the way to wonder, the gift of grace. There can be no fear when there is gratitude. No anger. No jealousy. No doubt. Thankfulness brings focus to the positive aspects of one's life. When one is grateful, one is *present*.

Focus on the small details, then expand to the broad concepts. There is much to be grateful for; fingers and toes, eyes and ears, heart and lungs, all work together in the marvelous system of the body. Even a body with illness has much that is still functioning well. Do not take for granted all that *is* right about the body.

> *"Think of all the beauty*
> *still left around you and be happy."*
> Anne Frank, *Jewish teenager in hiding during World War II*

Natural beauty is always a source of gratitude ~ for all the pleasure it provides, the healing of jangled nerves, the thrill of diversity, the nourishing bounty. The air we breathe, the water we drink ~ how often do we think about these basic needs that are met every day? As soon as they are damaged or scarce we realize what we never noticed ~ the miracle of the natural world that sustains us.

Our friends and family may seem a permanent feature in our lives, but they too are to be cherished. Life is fragile and can change in an instant. Being truly present means being grateful for each and every moment spent with those we love. Take in the sights and sounds as much as possible. Memorize the scene so that you enjoy all the blessings of relationship while they last.

Benefits of gratitude

Being in a state of gratitude makes all life easier to bear. Of course, difficulties arise ~ daily. How one responds to the challenges determines the quality of the experience. Anger, fear, distrust, and confusion take one to a low place emotionally and physically. Negative emotions cause great harm to the delicate systems of the body. The gut produces acids, the brain produces distress signals, the muscles tense, the heart races ~ all signaling danger is present. If the threat is real and imminent, flight is the necessary action. But if the situation is interpersonal conflict that is ongoing and must be endured, the results are inaction and internal stress. The continuous stressing of the systems eventually leads to low functioning and breakdown. Minute by minute our reality is built or destroyed. Self-pity leads to destruction.

Gratitude re-frames the picture. It focuses on the positive, unexpected outcomes of today's struggles. It lightens the load and affects those around the situation. Gratitude takes time to sink into. It is a practice and a goal. As with all routines, it will become easier over time to see everything through the lens of gratitude.

The benefits of gratitude are many for this attitude is helpful to all aspects of being. The mind benefits from positive thoughts, which bring about positive emotions, which lead to a healthy physical state. There can be no downside to this practice of viewing all things with the blessing of gratitude.

> *"Gratitude is not only the greatest of virtues but the parent of all others."*
> Cicero, philosopher

Each situation has the potential to create a positive ripple effect no matter how difficult it may seem at the moment. Whole movements of social causes have been built on individual tragedies. Group energy cannot be created without a catalyst. People are involved with their own daily lives and struggles until something jarring happens around them. A wake-up call is necessary to break through daily concerns. This call is often in the form of a tragedy, man-made or natural. The victim's loss touches the heart and troubles the mind, and the body moves to action. This is how it has always been. Progress is created through dissatisfaction with the status-quo. Our efforts are focused toward change for the better, through individual or group action. Therefore, even the worst of disasters can have the effect of moving humanity forward and upward.

Gratitude lightens one's load emotionally. Negative thoughts create a heavy burden to carry through the day. Anger and fear bring stresses that create turmoil in all systems.

Seeing the good in every moment keeps a balance in place. There truly is more good than bad to focus upon. The evening news, sad as it may be, is the worst that has happened in the world for the day. The rest of the story is that most people went about their day without incident.

Pleasure versus pain

Believe that all things work together for the betterment of humanity. Obviously pleasant situations are easy to praise for everything feels good and uplifting. Some of these very situations, however, lead one into trouble. Pleasant feelings do not always mean positive directions. Pleasure is a lure, a trap, a method of ensnaring the unaware. Better to be a bit uncomfortable and alert to the dangers that are present in the guise of pleasure.

On the other hand, discomfort, pain, and loss often produce amazingly good outcomes. Growth happens in these times of struggle. Inner strength is built from flexing the emotional muscles. Without resistance there can be no strength building. This is known in body building when considering muscles but also is true on the emotional, mental, and spiritual levels.

All opportunities for real growth come with resistance of some form. Pushing through the difficult times creates endurance and perseverance. Babies have little tolerance for resistance. They want everything *now!* Their ability to delay gratification is not yet formed.

Their distressed wailing signals to all that needs are not being met.

Maturity comes from the process of waiting for what is desired. Inner fortitude is built over time. The delays that aggravate us so are really building character and inner beauty.

Therefore, gratitude is always the appropriate response to all circumstances. The bright, delightful moments and the dark, fearful moments are working together to build a full, complete human experience. A life without pain would not be real or useful. This earthly experience is a complex learning journey of the soul. Welcome every day with gratitude for all that it teaches and all that it reaches, ever upward.

"Rejoice in the Lord always; again I will say, rejoice."
Paul, Apostle of Jesus

Take a breath

Gratitude allows us to breathe in deeply the simple delights of life. The beauty of a flower, the sweet sound of a bird's song, the patterns of a cloud-filled sky. This earth is so beautiful in all its diversity of form and color. Take time to spend in nature to open up the heart, calm the mind, and free the spirit. The natural world holds so much that brings a sense of awe if we take the time to study it. As scientists know, the deeper the look into any aspect of creation, the more marvels appear. The complexity of interconnected systems is astounding. Just the fact that we are living in the midst of such a wondrous, interdependent eco-system is a good place to start for a practice of gratitude.

"Be thankful for what you have; you'll end up with more. If you concentrate on what you don't have, you will never, ever have enough."
Oprah Winfrey, *media producer and philanthropist*

Breathing in this sense of gratitude brings well-being. Deeply exhale all tension and desires. Inhale what is already working in your life. Exhale places of struggle. The breath carries the feelings of peace throughout the body, relaxing and calming the chaos within. Liberate the natural state of well-being through the breath ~ truly the breath of a life well lived.

Focusing on the beauty in the natural world and the beauty in humanity is a beginning place for the practice of gratitude. For it is a practice, a habit to be formed. Pessimism is easy to fall into. Gratitude takes some effort.

Breathe in thankfulness. Breathe out peace.

With each breath we create harmony or chaos. Choose harmony. Release any tension as it arises through conscious breathing. Disperse the anxiety before it can become a hindrance to the body. Long, slow, deep breaths create a calming effect that benefits all aspects of health. God *is* breath ~ so breath *is* good.

A grateful heart is a full heart. Be open to all the bounties that surround you and the present will be a marvelous gift. And as each day passes into memory, a life of contentment will be created.

"It is through gratitude for the present moment that the spiritual dimension of life opens up."
Eckhart Tolle, *inspirational author*

The Lock on the Future:
F E A R

FEAR SAYS:

"Calamity is *just* around the corner."

"Failure will be very painful so I won't risk it.
I will stay *safely* inside what is known."

"I *won't* be able to cope with life's struggles."

"Why spend the time, the energy, the money?
I *won't* succeed anyway."

"Success is for smarter, prettier,
more talented people."

"The past is the template and the future will be
more of the same."

"Who am I to think I can create this new idea?
Who will listen to *me?*"

"I won't have enough…money, friends or family
to make it through life."

"Fear will *always* rule me. I can't be free of it."

"Fear is the strongest force in the universe."

FEAR

The lock on the future is fear.

Fear is the absence of hope. The future looks bleak when fear has a lock on one's hopes and dreams. Listening to the voice of fear stops all striving, for to strive *is* to hope for a better future.

There is no room for creative thinking when fear rules the mind. Only dark images come forth when negative thoughts abound. The seeds of invention need fertile ground to grow and thrive. Fear pours toxins onto the delicate shoots and they wither before they have a chance to bloom.

Fear stops risk taking and promotes playing it safe, but safety is an illusion. All of life is risky. We take a chance every time we leave our home. If fear totally has its way even that simple task becomes impossible. Some people are trapped by fear, and their own home becomes a prison. Fear can be felt but it must not be allowed to rule the day.

> *"Fear defeats more people*
> *than any other one thing in the world."*
> Ralph Waldo Emerson, transcendentalist poet

Fear limits options, ideas, and goals. Big thinking requires big actions and fear can stop *all* activity. Moving forward requires a hopeful energy, and fear can defeat the idea before it is even begun.

Fear is a contracting force on all levels. The body tightens at the first sign of fear ~ clenching muscles in the jaw, the gut, the neck. Breathing becomes shallow. Fingers and toes grip tight. The nervous system restricts information to preserve the status quo. The body tries to preserve energy. Real or just conjured up in the mind, the reaction to fear is the same.

The mind is scanning for threats all the time. Its job is to filter information and see patterns of dissimilarities which could cause trouble. The familiar is safe, and the new feels threatening because the new is unknown. The results could be wonderful or terrible, but the danger signal is sounded. The mind perceives potential harm from all sorts of unknowns ~ ethnic, religious, political, geographic, and occupational. Any time we step into a new situation, fear will be present to scan for trouble.

> *"A man who fears suffering*
> *is already suffering from what he fears."*
> Michel de Montaigne, French essayist

Fear can be protective, of course, in a situation of true bodily danger. The systems of the body react with fight or flight to keep one safe from natural disasters, war, and other real events. A gut feeling keeps you safe when judging new people or situations. And this needs to be trusted.

The problem arises when fear rules one's life, stopping any forward movement into unknown territory. Life is full of opportunities to try new things, meet new people, taste new foods. If fear is always the reason not to try something new, life is confined to a narrow band of experiences. The fear is perceived to be larger than the potential positive outcome. Fear can have such a tight grip on the mind that only familiar situations can be tolerated. *Different* and *new* become the enemies of peace and the safe world is small and known.

Fear clamps down on one's spirit. Adventure, excitement, novelty all are sacrificed to safety. A feeling of possibility is replaced with limitation. Creative ideas are met with doubt. Progressive plans are met with derision. Expansive concepts are met with skepticism. The sprit which loves to fly free is now captured in a very small cage of limited options. Fear confines and reduces life's possibilities.

> *"Of all the liars in the world, sometimes the worst are our own fears."*
> Rudyard Kipling, author

Fear is the restricting force of the universe. It stops positive action. It limits hope. It holds dreams captive. Fear never sleeps. It stalks the night devouring all who lie awake waiting for answers. The worst- case scenarios are envisioned and somehow become certainty in the dark hour's imaginings.

Fear lives on insecurity, past failures, lost chances, and poor decisions. It takes the past and projects it into the future, doubling down on the negative results. "Always" statements are a sign of fear. "I *always* try and fail." "I *always* come away disappointed." "I am *always* rejected." Fear loves those statements because they limit the possibility of new directions. It wants us to remain stuck in the pain of the past and fear of the future.

Fear is the source of doubt and clinging to old ways. Change, even when it is for the better, can be difficult to embrace. This is why we sometimes prefer our old ways to the new ones. Familiarity brings comfort. However, that very sense of comfort can stop us from receiving what we *truly* want.

Fear paralyzes creative action. Ideas still come, but moving forward with confidence requires faith. Fear lists the challenges, the hurdles, and the obstacles to success before the work has even begun.

> *"The brave man is not he who does not feel afraid, but he who conquers that fear."*
> Nelson Mandela, first black president of South Africa

Fear can disable the flow of positive outcomes envisioned through faith. Fear takes the energy out of hope and leaves deflated dreams. Fear elevates the doubts and reduces the possibilities of success. The power of fear is its ability to conjure up bad outcomes. In reality the possible outcomes are vast, from rousing success to crushing defeat and everything in between. Fear eliminates all but the worst possible situations and puts the focus there ~ on failure.

It takes courage to move forward with any new venture, from trying a new recipe to starting a business. Fear must be bypassed in order to let ideas grow. Losing is not the worst that can happen. Never trying is really the worst outcome. Fear takes life's forward motion and reverses the focus. It can lead to self-pity, which leads to regret. In order to live a full and varied life mistakes will be made, losses will come, failure will happen. To live under the thumb of fear is to be flattened, not fully formed.

> *"Do one thing every day that scares you."*
> Eleanor Roosevelt, First Lady and activist

Fear has great control in the area of money, for money is needed to make a life livable. Anxiety about the lack of money creates all sorts of negative situations. Believing in abundance helps make it so. And believing in lack stops the flow.

Something as simple as a quick prayer of gratitude for the bills being paid this month helps keep the flow coming. Choose a number and hold it in your mind as a goal for the year. Visualize that number on your year-end statements. Hold excitement for that outcome. And see what happens. Money can come from unexpected sources, not just your own labor. Expand your possibilities by expanding your goals.

Breathe in peace. Breathe out hope.

Keep fear under control through prayer, visualization, and breath. Often the breath ~ rapid and shallow ~ is an easy way to spot fear taking hold. Reverse the trend ~ deep breathing, conscious breathing will calm the nerves, slow the panic.

"Everything you want is on the other side of fear."
Jack Canfield, inspirational author

The Key
to the Future:
FAITH

FAITH SAYS:

"I live in confidence and I will be able to handle *whatever* comes my way."

"I know I am not alone. The Spirit of Guidance will be available always."

"My talents and gifts are enough to create success."

"I can always begin again. Past failure *does not* mean future failure."

"My intuition can be trusted to guide me through the day."

"Others' stories of faith can help me believe, too."

"I can *learn* from my struggles and grow stronger."

"I have been given dreams and desires to fulfill. I will *not* give up when times are difficult."

"What looks impossible and hopeless can be changed in a day."

"Love is the greatest power in the universe."

FAITH

The key to the future is faith.

Faith is the rock upon which we stand; an unshakable base which we build our lives upon. While others are tossed about with life's challenges, the person of faith stands secure; leaning into the winds of change but stabilized by the confidence that all is in order, believing in the Divine Wisdom that brings the best to us, although the form may be distressing.

Faith creates a bubble of protection from the emotional arrows that come our way. Those without faith are pierced by every dagger of doubt and confusion. Life brings challenges daily, and faith is the protective shield over the heart and mind. Fear's cold sword cannot cut through faith's breastplate. Faith is the divine gift that keeps us moving forward into an uncertain future.

> *"Now faith is the assurance of things hoped for,*
> *the conviction of things not seen."*
> A New Testament author

The future cannot be known as variables are always at play. Each person's free will allows constant adjustment to even the simplest plan. We often think we know what is in our future by extending today's situation. But anything can happen ~ good or bad ~ to create a totally different outcome. The future is a mystery to be welcomed, not feared. Living in faith allows today to be the stepping stone to tomorrow's contentment.

Believe it

Faith is belief in that which is not yet seen. For many this is impossible for they doubt all that cannot be touched. But for the faithful this is the way to happiness, fulfillment, and peace of mind.

When the future is a place of fear, one cannot manifest a bounty. Fear brings contraction and lack. Faith brings expansion and riches of all sorts ~ relationships, health, wealth, *and more faith.*

The practice of faith increases the results. The confidence in things that *will* be manifested brings about the very goals one seeks. For all is available in the realm of spirit ~ nothing is impossible. "If you have the faith of a mustard seed," as Jesus said "you can move mountains." This principle is just as valid today as when those words were spoken. And we have just as much trouble believing them now as his followers did then.

Imagination is the tool to bring faith into action. Seeing the positive results. Hearing the good news. Touching the solid form that we desire in our hearts.

Belief is necessary to create any new venture. We *believe* in the value of the idea. We *believe* in the systems we create to achieve the goal. And we *believe* in our ability to persevere till the end.

When all is set out before us the plan is clear, the goal is worthy, and the effort needed arises. This is how all change is manifested on the planet. To achieve one must believe. Action follows in the wake of a clear vision.

*Inspiration becomes manifestation
through perspiration.*

Dedicate your life to the process of receiving and achieving. It is the blessing of this realm that our bodies can achieve what our minds can conceive.

Inspiration

Listen for inspiration to guide you forward. The still small voice can be trusted to lead you safely through life's challenges. Although each person has to learn to discern the true voice of Guidance, there are common traits that can be sign posts.

In following the inner voice or intuition, a gut reaction is paramount. Circumstances bring the chill of fear for a negative outcome or the warmth of faith for a positive outcome.

Listen and observe the body's reaction to each new opportunity. The results are uncannily trustworthy. Blessings abound when faith is supreme. Faith involves listening to one's higher self for that is where faith resides. Longing for answers to our questions about the future presents itself as fear and worry. Listening to the inner still small voice which whispers, "Fear not, all is well," is a learned skill.

"Look in the heart…you will find the key."
Rabia Hunter, spiritual seeker and activist

Faith and accomplishment

Whenever doubt creeps into our mind, fear is sure to follow. How can we accomplish our goals, so lofty and distant? How can life take a positive turn when all seems bleak and hopeless? Where will the answers come from that will open the door to a new direction?

Everyone has these thoughts along the way to success. The key to that very success lies in faith overcoming fear. The inner struggle for confidence eclipses the outer actions every time. Belief brings relief when doubts plague the mind.

Faith is believing before receiving, holding onto a dream for the time that is takes to fully manifest. It may be minutes, days, weeks, months, years or a life time. Each goal has its own gestation period and it cannot be rushed into fulfillment. Small goals are achieved quickly and therefore are useful in creating momentum and confidence. Mid-sized goals build character and strength. Large goals build a life of achievement and satisfaction.

One who stays in the realm of small goals misses the opportunity to stretch and grow. Diligence, fortitude, and perseverance are needed for the large life-changing goals. And even with that effort, worldly success is not a guarantee. But personal growth is assured.

> *"An optimist takes the chance of losing;*
> *a pessimist loses the chance of gaining."*
> Hazrat Inayat Kahn, *Universal Sufi master and musician*

The choice of goals is, of course, critical to the outcome. Choose that which is lovely, helpful to others, and nurturing to self. Much effort spent going the wrong direction will still yield the wrong outcome. Heart, mind, and gut should be in agreement on any major challenge. To proceed without all three could spell disaster.

Staying positive

There are probable outcomes and possible outcomes and unexpected outcomes. The future is not yet written and faith can project a new reality of optimism. Listen for the hopeful news and build on that. Go for the long shot. Many have missed the mark, but some have made it. Be one who has tried and won.

See the outcome you desire. *Imagine* in vivid detail, all the aspects of your goal. Let your mind create a scene of happy resolution. Put yourself in the picture with a big smile on your face. This *is* faith ~ the ability to trust in the highest good and highest goals.

> *"Evolution and all hopes for a better world rest in the fearlessness and open-hearted vision of people who embrace life."*
> John Lennon, *musician and peace activist*

Opening to possibilities leads to unexpected results. There is more to be seen than meets the eye. Listen for guidance in the heart, the gut, and the mind. An urging to action, whether logical or not, needs to be followed. Logic is often the enemy of faith for it analyzes one out of taking action. *Move* in trust and the illogical becomes logical. *Wait* for understanding and the moment is lost.

Go forward without facts for the outcome will prove the path. When one is faithful to Guidance, Guidance is faithful to one. Following intuition creates an amazing life of miracles, coincidences, and remarkable perfect timing. To live without Guidance is to stumble around in the dark. Turn on the light of Faith and see the Path, illuminated before you.

Faith and healing

Healing especially depends on faith. When we open to the possibility of relief from suffering, the process begins. Doubt, of course, is the enemy of faith and good results. Doubt will drain the energy from our faith leaving us stuck in troublesome circumstances.

See the best, expect the best, be ready to claim the best outcome for yourself and others. Much has been lost from the lack of faith.

Fear binds. Faith releases.

Sending love to places of lack is like sending a healing balm. The body responds to love. Love is the beginning and end of the healing process. Without love, there can be no opening to change. Fear keeps conditions locked in place, tightly bound up, immovable. Fear amplifies pain. Fear multiplies loss. Faith opens up the possibility of healing.

Be open to the future

Leave all fear and doubt behind as you envision your future. There can be no better way to establish a positive outcome than to think positively. Success evolves from a seed of faith. Water the seed with confidence.

Nourish it with perseverance and harvest from a full grown tree of success. The process is slow and deliberate ~ not to be rushed. Give yourself the time necessary to achieve your dream. There is nothing worthwhile that arrives quickly. Work at the process daily and in small increments for eventually the harvest will be ready.

The future is the great unknown. Wonderful things can happen as well as tragedies. Uncertainty breeds anxiety and in reality much is uncertain. Even those who seem to have life in order can find all is turned upside down by an unexpected event. There are probable outcomes but not many certain ones. Learning to accept uncertainty and change brings peace.

We believe that knowing the future would bring peace, but actually it limits the possibilities. The future has flexibility when it is unclear. Good things can be added to the flow when there is openness and freedom. Knowing the ending ahead of time does not make the story more satisfying. The suspense adds to the experience. But one must stay hopeful and optimistic to bring about the best ending. Visualize a grand finale not knowing how the production will occur. Trust the One who is directing the play for the outcome in His hands. A big surprise always entails secrecy. Expect the best from the One who created the whole show.

"May your choices reflect your hopes not your fears."
Nelson Mandela, first black president of South Africa

61

Using the
Three Keys to
CONTENTMENT

USING THE THREE KEYS

How to use the keys daily

This is a pathway to work with every day until the responses are automatic. It is a practice of monitoring the thoughts that create unhappiness. Patterns of thinking can be observed and then altered to create release from negative emotions. Emotions follow thoughts and thoughts are in our control.

Rational thinking can be negative thinking in disguise. What is rational about hope, miracles, and inspiration? All the world's great minds, musicians, and artists have leapt into the unknown to seek their highest calling. Staying safely within boundaries may be rational but totally limiting. Listening to inner guidance takes us into uncharted territory where new worlds open up.

All that is known, of course, is already known. The *unknown* is where growth occurs. Experiment with your life. Push on the doors to see which ones swing open. Try all options. All is not revealed on the first day. A year is full of 365 new days to try again.

Persistence can wear down resistance.

This is a daily practice; minute by minute actually, for each moment forward creates a new past that needs forgiveness. Each moment is a new opportunity for accepting what is created now. And the future is always slipping forward, outside of one's grasp.

All that is known comes from these three stages of experience. Reality is nothing but moment to moment unfolding.

All that has gone before is dissolved into memory;
all that is hoped for is waiting in the ethers.

This moment is all that is real ~ then it too is gone. Unrelenting progress, moving forward, never back. This is the sanctity of life, the law of beginning without end.

Manifesting one's desires

Although hopes and dreams are crucial to manifest desires, so too is repetition. The thoughts that win are those that outnumber the rest. Over and over the message repeats and finally the results occur. As in advertising, repeating the message creates the sale.

You may not be aware of how often your thoughts are focused on the negative, the loss, the missing pieces. This guarantees the continuation of lack rather than abundance. Watch for repeating worries for they create a groove in the mind which is hard to overcome. Instead, focus on positive outcomes, no matter how distant, no matter how difficult to achieve. The very thought of success opens the channel to make it a reality.

Believing makes it so, doubting stops the flow.

Many have tried to create success from force of will. Use the force of repetition instead. As a single drop of water can wear away a rock, after years of repetition, so too can a thought wear away resistance. Success comes from persistent effort. Start with the mental effort, then move to the physical. You will have half the work done in the mind alone.

Perfectionism versus confidence

Letting go of notions of perfection releases one to enjoy what is available. Time has a way of erasing the details of the life we dreamed we would have and replacing it with an authentic one. Whatever is holding you back from truly creating a life of fulfillment needs to be released ~ old habits of negative thinking, limitations, doubts, and fears.

> *"Have no fear of perfection – you'll never reach it."*
> Salvador Dali, artist

Today we start anew with confidence in ourselves. Our ability to overcome obstacles is directly related to our confidence. Not all results are perfect in this method, but nothing can be accomplished with a defeated attitude. Let all achievement flow from the river of confidence.

Maybe you can *envision* a greater outcome than you ever thought possible. Hold onto the dream. Keep it close to your heart. Sharing with others can dilute the power of the process. What is growing needs the inner darkness until it is well formed. Revealing the tender shoots can cause them to wither under the light of scrutiny from others.

All artists know that there is a time to work alone and then a time to invite others to view the results. The vulnerable stage of creative beginnings is critical to a good outcome. Premature sharing risks the undermining of the whole project. Keep wise counsel with your own heart, your Creator, and perhaps a trusted teacher. You will know when the time is right, is ripe.

> *"For everything there is a season,*
> *and a time for every matter under heaven."*
> Solomon, Israelite king

Listening to the inner voice

There is a process available to all for gaining guidance on matters large and small. The way is simple, but it takes trust and practice to perfect the results. Some will question the source of the wisdom, others the wisdom itself, but there is no harm in this. Doubt sometimes leads to greater faith in the end.

Listening is a skill, an art, and a calling. Each time one practices, the channel is improved. Practice allows one to listen with a keen inner ear for the ever present voice of wisdom. Listen for the next word, write it down, listen again, and write again. The rhythm developed will carry you forward into new territory and surprising places. Listen without an agenda. Listen without a goal. Just listen and write what arises in the mind. There can be no better way to receive the Truth intended for you than to listen for the inner voice.

> *"My intuition, hast thou ever deceived me? No, never.*
> *It is my reason which so often deludes me, for it comes*
> *from without; thou art rooted in my heart."*
> Hazrat Inayat Khan, Universal Sufi master and musician

Outer sources all have their motives, their filters, their angles. Not that this is wrong for them, but it may not be right for you. Reading others' words is helpful but what is their source? Inner guidance or the workings of the mortal mind? Test with your own wisdom.

The voice of guidance

The Spirit of Guidance is available to everyone who truly listens. Many stories can be told of miraculous rescues and improbable inventions coming from this inner voice.

> *"Listen to yourself and in that quietude*
> *you might hear the voice of God."*
> Maya Angelou, poet, author, and teacher

Learning to cultivate a connection with this precious gift is paramount. Perhaps more important than anything we teach a child is to value the wisdom from within. Instead, children are told all the wisdom is external and they are only to follow the commands of others. This leaves children vulnerable to unscrupulous adults and peer pressure. A strong internal compass will guide a child through all sorts of dangers. A child who only follows can be led astray.

Listening to the *still small voice* takes practice and involves testing. Learn what a *Yes* feels like ~ energizing, uplifting, exciting or warming energy. If the answer is *Yes,* you feel the energy to accomplish the task. Experience a *No* ~ heavy, tired, cold, downward or chilling energy. If the answer is *No*, the task at hand feels like too much work.

We use this process all the time to make life's unending decisions on food, entertainment, and even life partners. It is easier to follow along when the results seem logical and practical. Everyday decisions can pull in facts from past experience, influence from advertisers, and personal desires. Guidance, on the other hand, can seem irrational. We are impressed to go in a direction that is totally unknown to us. By asking us to step out on faith, we increase the listening skill.

Inspired ideas

Inspiration is another form of guidance. Spontaneous and often unbidden, it delights us with its enthusiasm and positive energy. Everyone has experienced this form of listening to the Divine. It is not always thought of as a spiritual process, but one just has to look at the word *inspiration* to see that *spirit* is involved.

This experience cannot be controlled, only requested. We can ask for guidance, new ideas, and solutions, but answers will come in their own time and place. Many a solution arrives in a dream, for the mind is the most receptive when it is not actually focused on the problem. Countless stories are told of amazing answers to complex problems arising fully formed upon waking. Listening to these messages is easy because we see the cause and effect. We are seeking and we find, no matter how long the delay. This should give confidence to the listener that the inner receiver is working.

There is much to be gained from these impressions. This is how the world progresses in the Divine order, through inspired thought and holy action. Of course, dark thoughts also arise but these are not of the same source. The mind has the capacity to link information and create new ideas. Logic shows the way. The mind, not the heart, is in the lead. The world's horror also comes from creative thinking, sorry to say. Each person has the option to open the mind to high or low vibrations. Follow the high road.

Lessons learned from experience

The best teacher is life. We may read volumes of information, but until we experience the principles in action they remain ideas only. There is nothing to be gained from endless reading of directions ~ that does not get us to the destination. What is true in travel is true in life as well. Spiritual and personal growth concepts need to be implemented. Mere reading does not make us enlightened.

> *"A donkey carrying a load of holy books*
> *is still a donkey."*
> Traditional Sufi saying

Practice is what makes the difference and moves us forward along the path. Repetition is the tool to achieve the goal. Athletes know this, as do musicians, speakers, and advertisers. The repetition reinforces the message in the mind and the body responds in kind.

Belief in spiritual accomplishment requires faith in the art of repetition. The bane of piano students and spiritual seekers, the hard work of repetitive practice pays off in the end. No professional musician achieves their rank without practice. And the practice never stops until the musician's life is finished. To believe otherwise is childish wishing for success without the effort.

An athlete's ordeal to achieve their goal is even more strenuous, sometimes even life threatening. Bodily injury only temporarily detains the athlete. They push through rehabilitation and return to the struggle once more.

Why should achieving spiritual goals be any different? Belief and effort go together in the rising up of consciousness. Repetition creates a new groove in the mind that attracts results. Belief is helpful, repetition is necessary. Only though multiple impressions can results be truly transforming. A program of sustained mental action will create results. Of course those results can be positive or negative depending on the majority of the thoughts.

Blessings come to those who hold fast
to the image of blessings.

Practices to use

Imagination, breath and repetition start to change the emotions and inner landscape. The following suggestions will help to let go of the old and bring in the new. The more you use them the better the results.

A Breathing Practice

Visualize holding each key.
Repeat each phrase three times on the slow count of three.

⚷ The Past

Breathe out *Regret*   *from the lock of the mind*
Breathe in *Forgiveness* *from the key of the heart*

⚷ The Present

Breathe out *Self-pity* *from the lock of the mind*
Breathe in *Gratitude* *from the key of the heart*

⚷ The Future

Breathe out *Fear*   *from the lock of the mind*
Breathe in *Faith*   *from the key of the heart*

A Naming Practice

Visualize holding **The Key to the Past**
over your heart:

Name three people you can forgive.
Then add: *I forgive all the pains of the past*
and take three deep breaths.

Visualize holding **The Key to the Present**
over your heart:

Name three things for which you are grateful today
Then add: *I am grateful for all the blessings I have today*
and take three deep breaths.

Visualize holding **The Key to the Future**
over your heart:

Name three things that you desire for the future.
Then add: *I have faith in blessings in the future*
and take three deep breaths.

A Guided Visualization

Imagine you are handed an envelope with a note inside that says you have won the keys to your own life. To claim the prize you must go to the street address listed on the card. A doorman greets you and hands you three keys. He says the first key opens the basement door where you must enter.

You go down a set of steps to a door with a lock marked *Regret* and use your key marked *Forgiveness*. You open the door and see a crowd of people in the basement. You realize that you know them all: each one has done something that you resent, dislike, hate or even fear. To move up to the main floor, you need to forgive each person. As you do this they disappear until you are alone. A mirror hangs on the wall. You look at your own image and forgive yourself for all your failings and flaws. You exhale deeply and let it all go.

You climb the next set of steps to a lock marked *Self-pity* and use your key marked *Gratitude*. Inside this room on the main floor you see all the good things in your life now. Family and friends are there. Good food and fresh water. Access to knowledge and the freedom to use it wisely. An amazing body and opportunity to take care of it. You inhale deeply and take it all in.

Then you climb the final set of steps to the top floor where a lock is marked *Fear* and your last key is marked *Faith*. You enter this space full of large windows and you can see in all directions. Here are all the things you seek in the future ~ good health, wealth, and happiness. Great relationships. Job promotions. You inhale and exhale deeply, knowing that all things are possible.

Opening the doors to each level of consciousness reveals the inner workings of love.

Staying in the present moment

Do what you can now to improve the future. Release the past. But spend most of the day right here, right now. Stay on the ground floor of your emotional house as much as possible for maximum results.

Spiritual Community

Blooming roses need the proper soil to thrive and so we need community to give us the continuing nourishment to bloom into our special beauty. Spiritual friends encourage our spiritual life. They point us to the goal if we have strayed once more. They teach us by example how practices create a refuge amidst life challenges. They guide us toward beauty and away from life's coarser elements.

The community of friends is precious and profound for it creates a circle of protection in times of trouble. Leading the heart toward connection not isolation, we expand our personal power within the group.

Triple the strands of cord into a braid and the result is great strength. The same is true with people. Three can carry what would make one buckle under the weight ~ physically, emotionally, and spiritually. Together we can build great luminous centers of heart energy that radiate love to the world. Such centers have always existed on the earth, rising in intensity to a peak power, then fading out as another center takes over. All organisms have a life cycle, and groups do as well; from infancy to adolescence to adulthood and old age, the community lives its life.

We rejoice in the birth, struggle in the maturing process, revel in the full form, and grieve the decline. This is as it ever was; nothing is static, everything changes. We cannot stay still in any phase no matter how much we desire it.

Time moves forward always taking us with it into new chapters, new blessings, new challenges. To rejoice in all stages is the way of the saint. Mere mortals resist the changes or try to speed up the process. Neither tactic gives success for the pace is set, the rhythm beating steady.

Go forward on this journey together for the group experience will enhance your personal progress. Each strand strengthens the whole. Add your silver cord to the bundle of light that is created in sacred community.

The Light goes on even after the community has ended.
Love never dies.

Overcoming big challenges

Focus on the hopes and eliminate the fears from your mind every minute of every day. There is no possible gain from the fear mode. Nothing can be created from such dark matter. Fear is a vortex of energy that sucks you under its current. Many dreams have drowned in its undertow.

Believe that all things are possible. Solutions have been found to massive problems in the past. It can happen in the future as well. Creative minds will receive the guidance necessary to help humanity solve the earth's greatest challenges.

The outcome looks dire at this moment for we are on the edge of big change. The old way no longer works and the new path is not clear. This is the moment to push for the highest answers, the best outcomes, the brightest future. Blessings flow from the Source, just as love flows. There is a capacity to overcome all difficulty.

> *"These are the times that try men's souls."*
> Thomas Paine, *Founding Father of the United States*

These coming years will test the courage and integrity of each one of us. What are our true values? Where *do* we draw the line? What will we *not* compromise? What *will* we do for money? What will we *not* do for money? How *do* we work together to master the challenges presented? How *do* we bring together the needs and the resources?

Be willing to share. Be willing to change. Be willing to love.

Imagination and The Three Keys

Release your grip on reality and soar into the unknown. Imagination can take you into realms of enchantment where life is beautiful. Children know how to access this world of fantasy and joy. Watch their faces as they share what they see and hear. We become so serious and grounded in this outer world that we lose touch with the playful world within. Learn to listen for the call to whimsy once more.

We are born and we die.
And in between we color...
inside and outside the lines.

The mind can produce darkness or light, deprivation or abundance, hate or love. Use the power of purpose to concentrate the vibrations. See the same results that you seek for yourself, for *all* humanity ~ good health, a clean environment, loving relationships, and meaningful work.

"Logic will get you from A to B.
Imagination will take you everywhere."
Albert Einstein, physicist and mathematician

Blessings flow from one to another when we open the floodgates of love. *The Three Keys* open our hearts to the possibilities. A heart free of regret, self-pity, and fear can generate love of self and others.

See the possibilities. Use your keys.
Open the locks. Open the doors of the heart
to the blessings waiting there.

ACKNOWLEDGMENTS

My wise first readers:
Jan McGinley, soul sister,
for showing me the way forward.
Sarajane Williams,
for validation of the intuitive creative process.
Dennis Cleerdin,
for steady encouragement.
Rebecca McBride,
for skillful editing and proofreading.
Colin Rolfe and Paul Cohen,
for publishing expertise.

My family:
Sister Amy Yocom,
for love through our life journey together.
Brother Tim Rowe,
for believing in me.
Parents John and Marjorie Rowe,
for years of support and love.

All my generous teachers:
Those in body, including Yasmin Haut,
the talented heart of our community,
and those in spirit,
especially Samuel L. Lewis,
creator of the Dances of Universal Peace,
who changed the course of my life.

And finally, to the Spirit of Guidance
who saved my life.

"May the Message of God reach far and wide, illuminating and making the whole humanity as one single Family in the Parenthood of God."

Hazrat Inayat Khan, Universal Sufi master and musician